Who Is Teaching The Sunday School Teacher?

Five Ways God Forms Those Who Teach His Word

Dr. Benita Kay Hairston-Gorham, M.Div, D.Min, PhD Candidate

NEW BEGINNINGS CHRISTIAN PUBLISHER

HOPE MILLS – NORTH CAROLINA

© 2026 Benita K Hairston-Gorham

Unless otherwise indicated, all scripture quotations are taken from the New King James Version

Published by New Beginnings Christian Publishers (May 8, 2026)

Hope Mills, North Carolina

ISBN: 979-8-234-05069-4 (P)

ISBN: 979-8-234-05070-0 (E)

DEDICATION

This book is dedicated to every Sunday School Teacher who said yes to God before feeling ready, who stepped into the classroom with faith instead of confidence, and who continues to teach-not for recognition, but out of love for God and God's people. Your faithfulness matters more than you know.

TABLE OF CONTENTS

INTRODUCTION...1

HOW TO USE THIS BOOK.................................3

CHAPTER ONE: Formed By The Master Teacher: Jesus Christ...7

The Master Teacher captured attention......................13

The Master Teacher engaged with thought-provoking statements......................14

The Master Teacher gives space for reflection...........15

The Master Teacher created a transforming learning experience......................16

The Master Teacher captures attention 17

The Master Teacher brought God's word to life and spoke into the lives of his listeners 19

The Master Teacher engaged with contrast..................21

The Master Teacher spoke with confidence and care.23

CHAPTER TWO: Formed By The Indwelling Teacher: The Holy Spirit...26

The Holy Spirit is a helper 29

The Holy Spirit is a reminder 29

The Holy Spirit is a revealer.....................30

The Holy Spirit is an equipper 33

The Holy Spirit is a guide.....................34

No notes, just the Holy Spirit................................36

Faith in the Holy Spirit.....................................38

CHAPTER THREE: Formed Through The Gift Of Teaching...41

Discovering the spiritual gift 43

God's quiet work of formation 44

Confirmation of the call...................................46

The uniqueness of the teaching gift 48

The purpose behind the gift of teaching 52

The weight and responsibility of the calling to teach .55

CHAPTER FOUR: Formed By The Discipline Of Studying God's Word...61

The charge to study 63

Paul – Studying Scripture in light of Christ.................67

Stephen – A student of the Word....................70

Ezra – A studied Teacher 71

Peter – When study meets the Spirit................72

CHAPTER FIVE: Formed In Relationship: Learning From Those We Teach 75

Formed by what we see......................................77

Formed by what we feel.....................................81

Formed through hearing....................................83

CONCLUSION: The Teacher is Still Being Taught.......89

ABOUT THE AUTHOR 92

INTRODUCTION

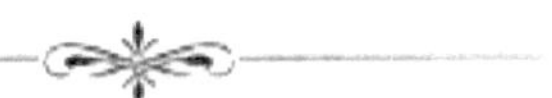

Have you ever sat in a Sunday school class and wondered, "Who taught this teacher?" For many years, I have been involved in Christian education as a teacher, secretary, superintendent, dean, and director, and one thing has become unmistakably clear: most Sunday school teachers are placed in their roles with little or no preparation. Some lack formal education, others are assigned to age groups they struggle to relate to, and many find it difficult to connect with students or present lessons in practical, meaningful ways. Yet, despite these challenges, many Sunday school teachers rise to the calling and profoundly shape the spiritual lives of their students.

How does this happen? If there is no formal training, then who teaches the Sunday school teacher? This book explores that very question by identifying five central ways teachers grow and develop: by following Jesus as the Master Teacher, by discovering the spiritual gift of teaching, by relying on the guidance of the Holy Spirit, by immersing themselves in Scripture, and by caring for every learner. As Parker Palmer (1998) reminds us, "Good teaching cannot be reduced to technique; good teaching comes from the identity of the teacher." The truth is that God equips Sunday school teachers in ways beyond human understanding, systems, and credentials, preparing them for the sacred task of shaping hearts and minds to build His kingdom. *What if the greatest teacher-training program is not a program at all, but a divine process initiated and guided by God Himself?*

HOW TO USE THIS BOOK

(A Formation Resource for Christian Educators)

This book was written to support the spiritual formation and faithful preparation of those who teach God's Word. While it may be read from beginning to end, it is intentionally designed for use in multiple settings.

1. **Individual Preparation and Reflection**
   - Teachers may use this book as a personal guide for prayerful reflection
   - Read one chapter at a time
   - Reflect on the themes presented in each chapter
   - Journal insights related to calling, growth, and teaching practice
   - Allow space for prayer and discernment between chapters

2. **Small Group Study or Teacher Cohort**
   - The book may be used within a group of teachers who meet regularly
   - Assign one chapter per meeting

- Encourage open sharing grounded in lived experience
- Emphasize listening, mutual support, and reflection
- Foster a sense of community among teachers

This format allows teachers to recognize shared challenges and affirm one another's calling.

3. Leadership Development and Mentoring

Church leaders, Directors of Christian Education, and ministry supervisors may use this book in mentoring contexts.

- Assign chapters to new or developing teachers
- Use discussion as a tool for discernment and support
- Pair reading with encouragement, observation, and feedback

This approach shifts teacher development beyond skill acquisition toward spiritual maturity.

4. Adaptation for Various Teaching Contexts

Although written with Sunday School teachers in mind, the principles in this book may be adapted for:

- Bible study leaders
- Youth and children's ministry workers

- Small group facilitators
- Christian educators in nontraditional settings

Leaders are encouraged to adapt the discussion and application to meet the needs of their context.

5. Five-Session Teacher Workshop (One Chapter per Session)

This book may also be used as a five-session workshop, with each chapter serving as the foundation for one session. Each is designed for approximately 60-90 minutes.

Session 1: Learning from the Master Teacher *(Chapter 1)*

> Focus: Jesus as the model for teaching and discipleship

Session 2: The Holy Spirit and the Teacher *(Chapter 2)*

> Focus: Dependence on the Spirit in preparation and teaching

Session 3: The Spiritual Gift of Teaching *(Chapter 3)*

> Focus: Teaching as calling, gifting, and responsibility

Session 4: Studying the Word Faithfully *(Chapter 4)*

> Focus: Approaching Scripture with integrity and humility

Session 5: Caring for the Learner *(Chapter 5)*

Focus: Creating learning environments marked by care and belonging

Looking Ahead: Facilitator's Guide

A facilitator's guide, including discussion questions and session-by-session guidance, is planned for publication in Fall 2026. This companion resource will support churches, educators, and training leaders in implementing the workshop format more fully.

CHAPTER ONE:
Formed By The Master Teacher:
Jesus Christ

"Did you know you're a very smart person?"

The question hung in the air like an unexpected gift, waiting to be unwrapped. I blinked, stunned, sitting in the office of my CPE supervisor during my Clinical Pastoral Education at WakeMed in Raleigh, North Carolina. The walls seemed to lean in, as if they too were waiting for my response, but all I could manage was a quiet, hesitant "No."

For someone who earned A's in school and loved every minute of it, you would think I would have seized the opportunity to agree. Instead, in that moment, I felt like an imposter. Smart? Me? The thought felt foreign, almost laughable. I remember thinking, "My doll babies might be smart, but not me." And yet, somehow, I was the one doing all the teaching.

As a child, teaching came naturally to me. I would rush home from school as my life depended on it, toss my backpack aside, and transform my bedroom into a classroom of eager students, or at least the students I imagined. I lined up my baby dolls across the bed, and without fail, I became the teacher of the year, delivering a full day's lesson whether they liked it or not.

They were smart doll babies, of course, but some struggled to follow the classroom rules. If one dared to talk too much or toppled face-first into the pillow, off to time-out they went. And homework? It was never turned in, no matter how many reminders I gave. Honestly, I had my work cut out for me, but somebody had to educate those students.

Even then, something about teaching stirred my heart. I did not fully understand why, but I was drawn to sharing what I knew and helping others "get it." I imitated the teachers I admired, repeating their phrases, mimicking their tone, and imagining what it might be like to stand before a real classroom one day. As the years passed, however, I came to see that the true model was Jesus. He is the one I now strive to emulate in every aspect of my teaching.

Jesus was, above all else, a teacher. While He healed the sick, cast out demons, and performed miracles that revealed His divine authority, much of His earthly ministry was devoted to teaching. Scripture consistently presents

Jesus as one who instructed, explained, invited questions, corrected misunderstandings, and patiently shaped the hearts and minds of His listeners. Teaching, for Jesus, was woven into daily life.

For Sunday school teachers and Christian educators, imitating the Master Teacher means paying close attention not only to what Jesus taught, but also to how He taught.

Luke gives us a glimpse of that model in Jesus' early years. *"After three days they found him in the temple, sitting in the midst of the teachers, both listening to them and asking them questions"* (Luke 2:46). Imagine the temple courts in Jerusalem during Passover, crowded, loud, alive with movement and debate. People fill the city. Teachers of the Law sit in familiar places, surrounded by learners eager to hear interpretations of Scripture. This is a space of serious study and deep tradition and, unexpectedly, a boy in their midst. He is twelve years old.

Luke tells us that after the Passover festival, Jesus stayed behind in Jerusalem while his parents continued, assuming he was among their relatives. Three days later, they found him in the temple, not wandering, not causing disruption, but seated among the teachers, listening intently, asking questions, and speaking with insight. Luke notes that *"And all who heard Him were astonished at His understanding and answers"* (Luke 2:47). When his parents finally approached him, both anxious and relieved, Jesus responded with words that reveal his inner orientation:

"Did you not know that I must be about my Father's business?" (Luke 2:49).

This pericope not only reveals Jesus' early engagement in listening and teaching, but it also lays the foundation for his growth. Luke records, *"And Jesus grew in wisdom and stature, and in favor with God and man"* (Luke 2:52). His childhood moment in the temple was not the culmination of his earthly teaching; it was the beginning.

That growth did not remain confined to sacred walls. As Jesus matured, his wisdom extended beyond the temple, beyond familiar spaces, and into the everyday places where people lived and worked. The boy who once sat among the teachers would become the teacher who walked among the people.

Jesus' mobility was an extension of his pedagogy. Matthew 11:1 states, *"Now it came to pass, when Jesus finished commanding His twelve disciples, that He departed from there to teach and to preach in their cities."* Teaching and proclaiming were not confined to a single place or audience. Once instruction was given, Jesus moved, entering towns, villages, shorelines, and homes to bring the message of salvation directly to the people. One encounter by the sea illustrates how Jesus transformed ordinary spaces into places of learning. Mark 4:1-2 records:

> *And again He began to teach by the sea. And a*
> *great multitude gathered to Him, so that He got*

*into the boat and sat in it on the sea; and the
whole multitude was on the land facing the sea.
Then He taught them many things by parables…*

Picture the scene. The shoreline is crowded, people pressing in, eager to hear him. There is no synagogue, no formal classroom, no scroll stand or raised platform. The water laps gently against the shore as Jesus steps into a small boat and sits down. From there, he faces the people, the breeze carrying his voice across the water. We are not in a building; we are outdoors, surrounded by fishermen, laborers, families, and the curious. Jesus looks at them not as a distant lecturer, but as one who knows their world. He begins to teach, not with abstract theory, but with stories drawn from their daily lives, seeds, soil, and harvest. The lake becomes his classroom, and ordinary life becomes the curriculum. Jesus' way of forming learners through presence, invitation, and everyday moments still shapes how teaching happens in the church today.

Imagine we have just arrived at church, rushing through the doors to the Sunday School Teacher's Seminar. We settle into our seats, waiting for the instructor to arrive. Five minutes pass. We glance at our watches, thinking, "The teacher is late." Just as we begin to wonder what is happening, the door opens, and in walks the Master Teacher himself, Jesus. There is no fanfare, no announcement, just Jesus. For the next sixty minutes, we watch him teach, not just any lesson, but one that unfolds before our very eyes. It is a story of a woman dragged before him in shame and a crowd poised to execute judgment. Watch how the Master Teacher captures attention, engages the audience, illustrates truth, and creates a transforming learning experience.

"Now early in the morning He came again into the temple, and all the people came to Him; and He sat down and taught them. Then the scribes and Pharisees brought to Him a woman caught in adultery. And when they set her in the midst, they said to Him, "Teacher, this woman was caught in adultery, in the very act. Now Moses, in the law, commanded us that such should be stoned. But what do You say?" This they said, testing Him, that they might have something of which to accuse Him. But Jesus stooped down and wrote on the ground with His finger, as though He did not hear. So when they continued asking Him, He raised Himself up, and said to them, "He who is without sin among you, let him throw a stone at her first." And again He stooped down and wrote on the ground. Then those who heard it, being convicted by their conscience, went out by one, beginning with the oldest even to the last. And Jesus was left alone, and the woman standing in the midst. When Jesus had raised Himself up and saw no one but the woman, He said to her, "Woman, where are those accusers of yours? Has no one condemned you?"

She said, "No one, my Lord," And Jesus said to her, "Neither do I condemn you; go and sin no more" (John 8:2-11).

In this pericope, we witness one of the most powerful teaching moments of Jesus' ministry. The scene unfolds with tension, accusation, and a crowd watching to see how he will respond.

The Master Teacher captured attention

Instead of responding immediately, Jesus stooped down and wrote in the dirt (v. 6). If that does not capture our attention, it is hard to imagine what would. It almost certainly captured the attention of everyone who had brought the woman to him. Questions likely surfaced in their minds. What is he thinking? What is he writing? Is he going to answer them? This unexpected silence draws everyone in, creating anticipation and tension as they wait for his response. It also shifts the focus away from the woman's sin and toward their own heart.

Now, if we are all teachers in the classroom, what does the Master Teacher show us? He shows us how to capture attention. Imagine a Sunday school teacher stepping into the classroom and introducing the lesson by saying, *"Today, we are going to step into one of the most intense moments in Scripture, where a woman is dragged before Jesus in shame, a crowd demands justice, and the Master Teacher responds in a way no one expects."*

The Master Teacher engaged with thought-provoking statements

Now we are sitting with anticipation. Jesus has captured our attention, and then the Master Teacher does something powerful. He makes a thought-provoking statement. Imagine the woman standing there in humility, the religious leaders holding stones in their hands, waiting for his verdict. Jesus is still writing in the dirt. Then he speaks a single statement that stops them in their tracks: *"He who is without sin among you, let him throw a stone at her first"* (v. 7).

Jesus does not ask a question. He makes a statement that causes them to ask a question of themselves. This is the Master Teacher at work. He does not accuse them, nor does he tell them what to do. He makes a statement that forces reflection. And notice, they say nothing. There are no arguments, no rebuttals, no excuses. One by one, they walk away, convicted.

As Sunday school teachers, can we shape a thought-provoking statement or question so powerful that students do not merely answer it, but reflect on it? A statement or question that lingers in their minds long after class is over. One that does not simply fill time, but leads to transformation. Imagine a Sunday School Teacher beginning this lesson by asking: *"We are often quick to judge others for their sins, but if our sins were exposed for everyone to see, how would we hope to be treated?"*

The Master Teacher gives space for reflection

The men walk away, and you might think the class is over, that the bell has rung, the case has been heard, and the prosecutors have dismissed the charges. Yet the woman remains, standing in humility, watching Jesus write in the dirt.

> *"Then those who heard it, being convicted of their conscience, went out one by one, beginning with the oldest even to the last. And Jesus was left alone, and the woman standing in the midst"* (v. 9).

As the men slip away one by one, Jesus' silence speaks louder than words. He remains bent down, his eyes fixed on the ground, never looking toward the retreating men or the woman standing before him. Then the sound of the final footsteps fades, and the last man turns and walks away. The hush is deafening. Only then does Jesus rise to his feet, meeting the woman's gaze as he finally speaks. Jesus straightens up and asks her, *"Woman, where are those accusers of yours? Has no one condemned you?"* (v. 10).

Notice that it is only after the final footsteps fade that Jesus stands up and speaks to the woman. In doing so, he shows how space creates room for reflection. He does not rush to fill the silence or explain the moment. Instead, he allows time for the lesson to settle. This reminds us that allowing students moments to pause, process, consider, and engage with the Scripture being shared can deepen understanding. Reflection gives meaning to what has been taught and transforms information into understanding, allowing it to take root in hearts and minds.

The Master Teacher created a transforming learning experience

Before we dismiss the class, let us take one final moment to reflect on how Jesus created a truly transformational learning experience. The accusers walked away, convicted by their own sin. The woman, expecting condemnation, instead experienced forgiveness and a new beginning. Those who witnessed the moment gained a new perspective on justice and mercy. In a single moment, Jesus did not simply teach a lesson; he changed lives, leaving his audience marked by an experience they would never forget.

Class dismissed. The Master Teacher walks out of the classroom.

The next day, Jesus returns to the classroom. This time, an open hillside serves as his setting. There are no stones, no accusers, no questions written in the dirt. Instead, Jesus opens his mouth and teaches, delivering a message that pierces hearts and transforms lives. So come with me. Let us take our seats among the crowd and watch as Jesus steps onto the mountain to teach.

The classroom is full again, every seat taken, and at the front stands an old wooden ladder. You slip into the last open seat, your eyes fixed on the ladder. Imagine for a moment that this classroom is the hillside where Jesus once gathered with the crowds. Instead of climbing a mountain, however, He climbs a ladder so everyone in the room can see and hear Him.

Then Jesus enters. The room grows quiet until the only sound is the rhythm of his footsteps. You notice the dust clinging to His sandals as He places His hand on the ladder and begins to climb. Higher and higher He goes, until every eye follows him upward. Finally, He reaches the top rung and sits down. From that place, elevated above the crowd yet close enough for every ear to hear, He pauses, looks across the room, and begins to speak.

Let us listen as Jesus speaks the words recorded in the fifth chapter of the book of Matthew.

The Master Teacher captures attention (v. 3-12, KJV)

Blessed are the poor in spirit: for theirs is the kingdom of heaven.

Blessed are they that mourn: for they shall be comforted.

Blessed are the meek: for they shall inherit the earth

Blessed are they which do hunger and thirst after righteousness: for they shall be filled

Blessed are the merciful: for they shall obtain mercy

Blessed are the pure in heart: for they shall see God

Blessed are the peacemakers: for they shall be called the children of God

Blessed are they which are persecuted for righteousness' sake: for theirs is the kingdom of heaven

Blessed are ye, when men shall revile you, and persecute you, and shall say all manner of evil against you falsely, for my sake

Rejoice, and be exceedingly glad: for great is your reward in heaven: for so persecuted they the prophets which were before you.

Jesus does not rely on performance or volume to gain attention. Instead, he captures attention with the very first words of the Sermon on the Mount. His calm authority commands the space. His opening words, what we now call the Beatitudes, are unlike anything his audience has heard. The listeners in his day expected power, but he spoke of meekness. They expected blessings tied to wealth or status, yet he blessed the poor, the mourners, and the persecuted. The contrast alone grips them, and the crowd leans forward.

Jesus uses the unexpected to capture attention, delivering a message that challenges assumptions. At times, it is not a loud voice or a polished presentation that draws students in. It is a surprising question, a story with a twist, or a truth stated freshly. Imagine a Sunday school teacher beginning this lesson by asking: *"What if being blessed does not look like success?"*

The Master Teacher brought God's word to life and spoke into the lives of his listeners (v. 13-16 KJV)

Jesus' teaching never floats above the heads of His listeners. He paints pictures with everyday things: salt and light, birds and lilies, a house built on rock or sand. These were objects and images His listeners encountered daily, and through them, He opened windows to their understanding.

> *"Ye are the salt of the earth: but if the salt have lost his savor, wherewith shall it be salted? It is thereforth good for nothing, but to be cast out, and to be trodden under foot of men"*

> *"Ye are the light of the world. A city that is set on a hill cannot be hid. Neither do men light a candle, and put it under a bushel, but on a candlestick; and it giveth light unto all that are in the house. Let your light so shine before men, that they may see your good works, and glorify your Father which is in heaven"*

In those few words, His followers could imagine the sharp taste of salt, the steady glow of a lamp, and the city gleaming on a hilltop. People knew that salt was not just for seasoning; it was also used to keep food from spoiling. When Jesus spoke of salt, they could connect it to preserving the truth of God's word and holding His teachings in their hearts.

Imagine a Sunday school teacher who holds up a small lamp as the room grows dim and says, *"This is what it looks like when one light shines and changes everything around it, just as one person can make a difference in a dark world or a dark environment."*

In the next chapter, Jesus speaks about worry, touching the places where their hearts wrestled in silence, the places no one else could see but God:

> *"Therefore, I say to you, do not worry about your life, what you will eat or what you will drink; nor about your body, what you will put on. Is not life more than food and the body more than clothes? Look at the birds of the air, for they neither sow or reap nor gather into barns; yet your heavenly Father feeds them. Are you not of more value than they?"* (Matthew 6:25-26)

Jesus knew there were people in the crowd who worried about food for their families and clothing for their children. He pointed to the birds of the air and the lilies of the field, both sustained by God, reminding them that they, too, were under His care. Their needs were not invisible to Him. Imagine a Sunday school teacher beginning this lesson on God's provision by asking: *"What worries keep you up at night?"*

Still later in chapter seven, He spoke of foundations:

"Therefore whosoever hears these sayings of Mine, and does them, I will liken him to a wise man who built his house on a rock: and the rain descended, the floods came, and the winds blew, and beat on that house; and it did not fall, for it was founded on a rock. But everyone who hears these sayings of Mine, and does not do them, will be like a foolish man, who built his house on the sand: and the rain descended, the floods came, and the winds blew and beat on that house; and it fell. And great was its fall" (Matthew 7:24-27).

His listeners knew what shifting sand could do to a house in a storm. They did not need a commentary; they could see it in their minds. It was something they understood through their everyday lives. Imagine a Sunday school teacher beginning this lesson with a statement: *"Storms do not create foundations; they reveal them. Today, we will examine the two foundations Jesus describes in Matthew chapter seven."*

The Master Teacher engaged with contrast (Matthew 5:21-44)

As Jesus continues in chapter five, He deepens the lesson with a pattern that shakes the listeners of His day's traditional interpretation: "You have heard that it was said…But I say to you."

"Ye have heard that it was said to those of old, You shalt not murder… but I say to you that whosoever is angry with his brother without a cause shall be in danger of judgment" (vss. 21-22).

"You have heard that it was said to those of old, You shalt not commit adultery….but I say unto you, that whoever looks at a woman to lust for her has already committed adultery with her in his heart" (vss. 27-28).

"You have heard that it was said, 'An eye for an eye and a tooth for a tooth.' But I tell you not to resist an evil person. But whosoever slaps you on your right cheek, turn the other to him also" (vss. 38-39).

"You have heard that it was said, You shall love your neighbor and hate your enemy. But I say to you, love your enemies, bless those who curse you, do good to those that hate you, and pray for those who spitefully use you and persecute you" (vss. 43-44)

This pattern of contrast immediately captured attention because it confronted deeply ingrained beliefs and long-held interpretations of the Law. Rather than affirming what religious leaders had taught the people, Jesus turned their understanding upside down, forcing them to reconsider what they had accepted as true. This shift was not only startling; it was impossible to ignore. His words disrupted familiar patterns of thinking, compelling listeners to question whether they had truly understood God's commands. In doing so, Jesus ensured that his message was not merely heard but actively engaged, leaving his audience challenged, captivated, and compelled to respond not just emotionally, but with a transformation in how they thought, interpreted, and lived. His words pressed them to reexamine both what they believed and why.

Sunday school teachers can ask questions that do not accuse but provoke reflection, gently inviting students to wrestle with truth and apply it personally. Imagine asking, *"Is what we practice today rooted in Scripture, or is it simply tradition?"*

The Master Teacher spoke with confidence and care

Throughout the teachings we now call the Beatitudes, Jesus' tone carried both authority and compassion. He did not speak like the scribes, quoting traditions or guarding inherited interpretations. Instead, He spoke with a clarity that flowed from intimacy with the Father and a deep awareness of the people standing before Him.

> *"And so it was, when Jesus had ended these sayings, that the people were astonished at His teaching, for He taught as one having authority, and not as the scribes"* (Matthew 7:28-29).

His confidence was not arrogance; it was assurance, rooted in the Word of God. Yet the same voice that declared, *"Love your enemies, bless those who curse you…"* (Matthew 5:44) also extended comfort: *"Blessed are those who mourn, for they shall be comforted"* (Matthew 5:4). Jesus' listeners felt both the weight of conviction and the warmth of His care. His teaching was firm enough to challenge but gentle enough to heal.

As Jesus concludes this chapter with love for our enemies, He steps down from the ladder. The room is still. Not a hand is raised. Not a question is whispered. The silence is not from confusion but from awe. People are absorbing what has just been spoken, words that pierced hearts, shifted thinking, and shaped lives.

This is the power of His teaching. Jesus' words captured attention, engaged through contrast, made truth understandable, connected to real life, and were delivered with confident love. When Sunday school teachers place their lessons in His hands and rely on His guidance, the classroom becomes more than a place of learning; it becomes a space of transformation. What happens there is not our work alone but His. So, who is teaching the Sunday school teacher? The answer is clear: the Master Teacher Himself. That is why the greatest training program is already in motion, facilitated by God.

 Lord, thank you for shaping and molding me through every teacher and every life experience. As I follow the Master Teacher, help me to teach with His heart, listen with compassion, speak with grace, and lead with love. Amen

CHAPTER TWO:
Formed By The Indwelling
Teacher: The Holy Spirit

"You Need to Talk in Class"

In grade school, I often got into trouble for talking in class, not because I was trying to be disruptive, but because I had already finished my work and was bored. While others were still working, I was ready to move on, so I started talking. My teacher would give me that look and say, "Benita, be quiet," and I would try… for a little while. But before long, the talking would start again. More than once, I was sent home with a sealed envelope tucked inside my backpack. My mother would open it and remind me not to talk so much. Still, I kept talking.

Then one day, everything changed.

I was in the middle of whispering to a friend when the classroom suddenly fell silent. Confused, I turned around, and there she was, my mother, standing at the front of the room. The look on her face said it all. Moments later, we stepped into the hallway, and I received a stern talk, not out of anger, but out of love and correction. That conversation became a defining moment in my life.

From that moment on, my voice disappeared in the classroom. I remained quiet as a church mouse through middle school, high school, and even my university years. If anyone knew I was in the class, it was only because of the papers I turned in. That conversation didn't just mean "stop talking"; it meant "be silent in a learning environment." It instilled the belief that silence was expected whenever I entered a classroom. But as a lifelong learner with a calling to teach, silence was never truly an option.

Years later, in my forties, I took a class at a Bible institute. After submitting a paper, the feedback read, "You need to talk in class." The words struck me, but I brushed them off. "Talking is not for me." A few years later, while attending seminary, a classmate leaned over and whispered, "The professor expects you to speak." The old fear came rushing back. Then came the moment I dreaded. I was assigned to read a parable aloud in class. My voice trembled as if I were crying, and my heart raced. The fear that had been planted so long ago was still there.

But this time, something was different.

I remembered the promise of 2 Timothy 1:7: "*For God has not given us a spirit of fear, but of power and of love and of a sound mind.*" That verse gave me the courage to push through. My mother was no longer there to silence me. I realized it was not just about finding my voice; it was about answering the call to speak and to teach.

The enemy had tried for years to keep me silent, but the Holy Spirit continually reminded me that I was never alone. Romans 8:26 reminds us: "*Likewise the Spirit also helps in our weaknesses...*" Even when fear lingered, the Holy Spirit gave me the boldness to walk in the calling God placed on my life. What I experienced in that moment was not unique to me; it reflects the Holy Spirit's ongoing work throughout Scripture.

From the beginning of creation, the Holy Spirit has been active. In Genesis 1:1-2, we read, "*In the beginning God created the heavens and the earth. The earth was without form, and void; and darkness was on the face of the deep. And the Spirit of God was hovering over the face of the waters.*" The Spirit of God hovered over the waters, participating in God's creative work. In the New Testament, Jesus teaches that new life requires the work of the Holy Spirit: "*…unless one is born of water and the Spirit, he cannot enter the kingdom of God*" (John 3:5). The same Spirit who gave life at creation now provides spiritual life through rebirth.

The Holy Spirit is a helper

It was the Holy Spirit who empowered me to overcome years of silence. Though I had been taught the Word of God, I still needed help remembering it and applying what I had learned. John 14:26 begins by saying, *"But the Helper, the Holy Spirit…"* Jesus described the Holy Spirit as the Helper, one who comes alongside God's people in their weakness, uncertainty, and calling. In John 14:16, Jesus promised, *"I will pray the Father, and He will give you another Helper, that He may abide with you forever."* The word Jesus uses points to one who supports, strengthens, and stands beside another. The Holy Spirit helps teachers navigate difficult questions, sensitive conversations, and moments when words seem inadequate.

The Holy Spirit is a reminder

John 14:26 continues by stating that the Holy Spirit would *"remind you of all that I have said unto you."* For the Sunday school teacher, this reminder function operates both within and beyond the instructional moment. It is present during teaching, in response to students' inquiries, and even after formal instruction has concluded. Such moments of recall are not spontaneous events detached from preparation. Rather, they emerge from sustained and intentional engagement with Scripture over time.

Time spent studying, memorizing, and meditating on the Word is never wasted. Through these formative practices, Scripture becomes internalized, and the Holy Spirit draws from what has been stored within, bringing it forward when it is most needed to guide both teacher and learner. A teaching of Jesus surfaces during a discussion. A once forgotten passage suddenly brings clarity to confusion. These moments are not coincidences. They reflect the Spirit's ongoing work of forming the teacher and guiding the act of teaching.

The Holy Spirit is a revealer

Scripture affirms that God is the one who reveals what is hidden and beyond human understanding. As Daniel 2:22 declares, *"He reveals deep and secret things; He knows what is in the darkness."* This revealing work is not rooted in human intellect but in divine initiative. That truth is vividly illustrated in the Old Testament narrative of Joseph, when a palace is quiet, but far from peaceful:

> *Then it came to pass at the end of two full years that Pharaoh had a dream; and behold, he stood by the river. Suddenly there came up out of the river seven cows, fine looking and fat; and they fed in the meadow. Then behold, seven other cows came up after them out of the river, ugly and gaunt, and stood by the other cows on the bank of the river. And the ugly and gaunt cows ate up the seven fine looking and fat cows. So Pharaoh awoke. He slept and dreamed a second time; and suddenly seven heads of grain came up on one stalk, plump*

and good. Then behold, seven thin heads, blighted by the east wind, sprang up after them. And the seven thin heads devoured the seven plump and full heads. So Pharaoh awoke, and indeed, it was a dream (Genesis 41:1-7).

Pharaoh has been shaken awake by dreams that refuse to release him. Night after night, the images return: cows rising from the Nile, ears of grain bending in the wind, abundance followed by devastation. The wisest men of Egypt have spoken, yet their words fall flat. No interpretation satisfies. Their wisdom reaches its limit, and the silence that follows is heavy with uncertainty.

Now it came to pass in the morning that his spirit was troubled, and he sent and called for all the magicians of Egypt and all its wise men. And Pharaoh told them his dreams, but there was no one who could interpret them for Pharaoh (Genesis 41:8).

Then Joseph enters. He is not dressed like the others. He carries no symbols of authority and no polished confidence shaped by power. He comes straight from a prison cell, summoned suddenly into the presence of the most powerful man in Egypt. The room watches him closely. Pharaoh speaks first, recounting the dreams once more, hoping this man will succeed where all others have failed.

Joseph listens. He does not interrupt. He does not rush to prove himself. When he finally speaks, he makes it clear that the insight does not originate with him: "*….It is not in me; God will give Pharaoh an answer of peace*" (Genesis 41:16). Joseph's discernment was possible only because God chose to disclose what would otherwise remain unknown. The interpretation unfolds with clarity: years of abundance, years of famine, a warning wrapped in mercy. Pharaoh then turns, not only to Joseph but to those standing near him, and asks, "*Can we find such a one as this, a man in whom is the Spirit of God?*" (Genesis 41:38).

While the Old Testament does not yet articulate this work in fully developed pneumatological language, the New Testament makes explicit what was previously implicit. The apostle Paul writes:

> *"But as it is written, Eye has not seen, nor ear heard, nor have entered into the heart of man the things which God hath prepared for those who love Him. But God has revealed them to us though His Spirit. For the Spirit searches all things, yes, the deep things of God."* (1 Corinthians 2:9-10)

This Scripture affirms that the Holy Spirit continues the work of revelation, enabling Sunday school teachers to discern, understand, and communicate God's Word as they depend on Him rather than on their own expertise.

The Holy Spirit is an equipper

God does not merely call individuals to serve; He equips them for the work they are given.

Throughout Scripture, the work of the Holy Spirit is not limited to guidance or inspiration alone. The Spirit actively supplies what is needed for faithful service.

One person we might easily overlook in Scripture is Bezaleel. Yet, he is one of the few individuals about whom the Bible explicitly states that he was not only filled with the Spirit of God but also equipped with wisdom, understanding, knowledge, and a wide range of skills. In Exodus 31:1–5, the Lord tells Moses:

> *Then the Lord spoke to Moses, saying, "See, I have called by name Bezalel the son of Uri, the son of Hur, of the tribe of Judah. And I have filled him with the Spirit of God, in wisdom, in understanding, in knowledge, and in all manner of workmanship, to design artistic works, to work in gold, in silver, in bronze, in cutting jewels for setting, in carving wood, and to work in all manner of workmanship.*

Bezaleel was appointed by God to oversee the construction of the tabernacle. His calling required precision, creativity, organization, and faithful execution, all of which were empowered by the Spirit rather than by human talent alone.

Scripture further explains that the Lord equipped Bezaleel not only with personal skill but also with the capacity to work alongside and instruct others:

> *"And I, indeed I, have appointed with him Aholiab the son of Ahisamach, of the tribe of Dan; and I have put wisdom in the hearts of all gifted artisans, that they may make all that I have commanded you"* (Exodus 31:6).

> *"And He has put in his heart the ability to teach, in him, and Aholiab the son of Ahisamach, of the tribe of Dan"* (Exodus 35:34).

Notice that the Spirit's equipping extended beyond craftsmanship to instruction, collaboration, and leadership. Bezaleel's experience affirms that skill, preparation, and teaching ability are sacred gifts when they are empowered by the Spirit and offered in obedience to God's call.

The same Spirit who revealed dreams to Joseph and equipped Bezaleel for leadership will later send, guide, and speak through others in unexpected places, on desert roads, in quiet conversations, and in moments that seem ordinary until the Spirit moves.

The Holy Spirit is a guide

In addition to revealing and equipping believers for service, the Holy Spirit also guides God's people step by step. This guidance is often quiet and unexpected, leading individuals away from familiarity and certainty and into moments of divine purpose. Now imagine this moment with me as we watch Philip leave the service and step onto the dusty desert road stretching from Jerusalem to Gaza (Acts 8:26-39).

The sun beats on our backs, the air is still, and all seems ordinary, until the Spirit of God begins to move. Ahead, we see Philip, one of the first deacons of the church, a man who has just been preaching revival in Samaria. Now, at the Spirit's command, he has left the crowds and proceeds down a lonely road.

As we walk with him, we see a chariot approaching in the distance. Inside rides an Ethiopian eunuch, a man of influence and education, carefully reading from the prophet Isaiah. His lips form the words, but his face shows confusion. Just then, the Spirit whispers to Philip: *"Go near, and join thyself to this chariot"* (Acts 8:29, KJV). Obediently, Philip moves closer and hears the eunuch reading aloud. Then comes the Spirit-led question: *"Do you understand what you are reading?"* (Acts 8:30). The eunuch looks up, almost with relief, and answers honestly: *"How can I, unless someone guides me?"* Here is the moment where the Spirit's guidance and the teacher's calling meet. The Spirit led Philip to the right place, at the right time, to meet the right need. It is not a coincidence; it was a divine appointment.

Philip climbs into the chariot, and the eunuch invites him to explain the Scripture. Led by the Holy Spirit, Philip begins with Isaiah and tells him about Jesus. This is the same Spirit Paul describes in 1 Corinthians 2:10-11, the Spirit who reveals the deep things of God and gives us the words to teach. The eunuch could not understand until a Spirit-filled teacher came alongside, and Philip could not teach apart from the Spirit's illumination.

Their travel in the chariot continues until they come upon some water. The eunuch, moved to faith, asks to be baptized. They stop the chariot, Philip baptizes him, and the eunuch goes on his way rejoicing. This is the work of the Spirit, not only guiding the teacher and giving understanding, but also equipping the moment for transformation.

No notes, just the Holy Spirit

And it is this same Spirit that empowers the delivery of what has been revealed. What begins in revelation finds its expression in proclamation. This is seen in the life of Peter, an ordinary man who stood before the crowd at Pentecost with no notes, no script, and no hesitation, speaking as the Spirit gave him utterance.

Go with me to Jerusalem, a city alive with festivities, crowds filling the streets, merchants calling their prices, families celebrating the Feast of Weeks. Yet in the upper room, something is happening that will alter the world. A sudden sound, like a rushing, mighty wind, sweeps through the house where the disciples are gathered. Cloven tongues like flames of fire appear, resting upon each of them, and the people in the city erupt in confusion.

Then one steps forward: Peter, once unsure and afraid, now filled with the Spirit, stands to speak with boldness, not from natural courage, but from divine empowerment.

> *"But Peter, standing up with the eleven, raised his voice, and said to them, "Men of Judea and all who dwell in Jerusalem, let this be known to you, and heed my words. For these are not drunk, as you suppose, since it is only the third hour of the day. But this is which was spoken by the prophet Joel: And it shall come to pass in the last days, says God, That I will pour out of My Spirit on all flesh; Your sons and your daughters shall prophesy, Your young men shall see visions, Your old men shall dream dreams:…..And it shall come to pass, that whoever calls on the name of the Lord shall be saved"* (Acts 2:14-17, 21)

Peter begins to interpret what the people are witnessing. Without turning pages, referencing commentaries, or consulting notes, he reaches back to Scripture to bring clarity in the moment. Like Philip, Peter does not teach in his own strength but yields to the Spirit, who empowers him to teach others.

For Sunday school teachers, the Holy Spirit is not optional; He is essential. Teaching Scripture is not merely the transfer of information; it is participation in the work of God. The same Spirit who guided Joseph, empowered Bezaleel, led Philip, and spoke through Peter now works in those who teach God's Word. This continuity reminds us that the Spirit's work in Scripture is inseparable from the Spirit's work in teaching. If the Scriptures were written by men inspired by the Holy Spirit (2 Timothy 3:16), then we must also rely on that same Spirit to teach us as we teach others. Without the Spirit, lessons risk becoming information without transformation. With the Spirit, the Word becomes living and active, cutting to the heart and giving life.

Faith in the Holy Spirit

However, to lean on the Spirit in this way requires faith. Teaching under the guidance of the Holy Spirit means trusting Him to bring the right words to mind at the right time. If God is the one who gives life to our message, then we must believe that the work of the Holy Spirit is greater than our preparation. Faith reminds us that we are not the source; we are simply the vessels. It is faith in the Holy Spirit that sustains the teacher when the lesson feels uncertain or when hearts appear unmoved. Faith is what keeps the Sunday school teacher standing, believing that God's Word will reach its mark even when we cannot see the results.

When I think about faith, I remember my mother. She was a brilliant woman who graduated with honors as a registered nurse during a time of racial injustice. When asked what words she wanted beneath her yearbook picture, she chose: "Have Faith." Her life reflected that conviction. She faced obstacles yet leaned on God for strength. In the same way, every Sunday school teacher must have faith, not in their ability to craft the perfect lesson, but in the Spirit who breathes life into every word spoken and every truth taught.

Every morning, as I step into my study, the first picture I see is of my mother, and the first words I read are "Have Faith." Those words steady me as both teacher and servant of God, reminding me that the Spirit who breathed life into Adam, who empowered Philip on the desert road, is the same Spirit who breathes into me today, giving courage to teach, strength to serve, and faith to endure.

In the end, the greatest teacher training is not found in manuals or methods, but in learning to listen to the Spirit of God. Just as the Holy Spirit guided Philip to the Ethiopian eunuch, He continues to guide Sunday school teachers today, showing us where to go, what to say, and how to teach. When we follow the Holy Spirit, our teaching becomes more than our work; it becomes His work through us.

So, who is teaching the Sunday school teacher? The answer is clear: the Master Teacher Himself, working through the Holy Spirit.

Thank you, Macieon L. Redd-Hairston, Mom, for constantly reminding me to have faith, not in my ability, but in the one who imparted the gift of teaching.

CHAPTER THREE:
Formed Through The Gift Of Teaching

"Your destiny is decided by God, but the fulfillment is decided by you," Dr. Myles Munroe.

Here I go, another Sunday, walking up the stairs to the balcony. Other kids would pass me, giggling, as if this were their chance to escape their parents, a place to hide so they could talk and play. I would go up there to sit in the front, making sure no one blocked my view when the pastor stood to preach. I tuned out everything else, my eyes and ears fixed entirely on the preaching moment.

When the church service ended, and I walked the three blocks home, I would rehearse what the pastor said, knowing that as soon as I opened the door, my father would ask, "So what did the pastor preach about today?" He asked the question every week, making sure I had been paying attention during the sermon.

I can't recall ever seeing my father in church, but every week he would sit in front of the television, watching Jimmy Swaggart and Billy Graham. I was the only one attending this particular church at the time. My parents didn't go regularly, and my sister attended church with her friends. I don't recall my father ever asking my sister that question, perhaps because her friend's father was the pastor, and he assumed she was listening and behaving in church.

Nevertheless, I would change my clothes, grab a comb, and jump onto the back of the couch. As I parted my father's hair and brushed away the dandruff, I would begin: "Now, Dad, the pastor said, open your Bible to Psalm 121, verse 1. His subject was 'God is a present help.' He said God is always there to help us." Then he went down a list of people in the Bible whom God helped. He said, "God helped Sarah when she could not have a baby. He helped Daniel in the lion's den, and he explained what happened to Daniel. He said God helped Shadrach, Meshach, and Abednego." Everyone laughed when he went back and said, "Shadrach, Meshach, and a bad Negro." Then he talked about how God helped Moses cross the Red Sea, how God had sent Moses to… So, Dad, I noticed that every time the pastor comes to the end of his sermon, he talks about Jesus, and people stand up. Today, he said, "Jesus died and sent down the Holy Spirit to help us and to give us the power to overcome anything we are going through…"

Looking back on my experience with my first student, I realize that we may unknowingly use our gifts long before we fully recognize them. My early teaching experience was not something I initially identified as a gift, yet it revealed a natural ability that God had already placed within me. Often, we act in ways that reflect the spiritual gifts we have been given, even if we do not yet understand their divine origin.

Discovering the spiritual gift (often before we name it)

Many teachers begin using their God-given gifts long before they recognize them as such. These gifts show up in small, ordinary ways: helping a younger sibling with homework, leading devotionals, teaching doll babies, explaining a Bible verse in Sunday school, or finding joy in showing someone how to do something new. At the time, it may feel like "just what I do" or a reflection of one's personality. Yet beneath the surface, God is shaping and preparing a Sunday school teacher.

Over time, what first appears as something natural is revealed as a sacred calling already taking shape. Teaching that once felt like "helping out" or "filling in" gradually emerges as the earliest expression of a spiritual gift already at work. Calling is rarely revealed all at once; it unfolds as God opens our eyes to the good work He has already begun: *"Being confident of this very thing, that He who has begun a good work in you will complete it until the day of Jesus Christ"* (Philippians 1:6).

Yet formation does not always come with immediate awareness, and sometimes the hardest person to see is the one God is calling us to become. It is often easier for others to recognize a teaching gift than it is for the one who carries it. Affirmations from mentors, peers, or leaders frequently serve as mirrors through which God reveals what we have not yet seen in ourselves. Think about the boy who loves gathering friends to share stories, or the young woman who is constantly learning and eager to teach what she knows. To them, it may feel ordinary. To those watching, it looks like something more. These moments are not accidents; they are glimpses of God's workmanship. As Ephesians 2:10 reminds us: *"For we are His workmanship, created in Christ Jesus for good works, which God prepared beforehand that we should walk in them."*

God's quiet work of formation

Divine calling is usually preceded by a season of quiet, unseen formation. This shaping rarely happens all at once; instead, it unfolds gradually through life experiences, seasons of growth, and moments of preparation that may not initially appear connected. God uses these hidden seasons to cultivate character, deepen understanding, and build dependence on Him. What may seem like unrelated experiences is often part of God's intentional process of shaping the teacher from the inside out.

When we look more closely, these experiences reveal how God uses the ordinary details of life to prepare us. He draws on past lessons, struggles, and moments of growth to prepare teachers for future responsibility and service. One of my favorite figures in the Bible, whom I think of when reflecting on spiritual calling, is the prophet Jeremiah. His assignment was not merely to speak, but to become a living message. God called him to communicate in ways that capture attention and stir hearts.

Picture the crowded marketplace as Jeremiah arrives, carrying a clay jar. People glance curiously, whispering, "What is he doing?" Without warning, he throws the jar to the ground. It shatters, the crash echoing through the square. Gasps fill the air as Jeremiah's voice cuts through the chaos: just as the jar was broken beyond repair, God would shatter Judah for its unfaithfulness (Jeremiah 19:10-11). The message is as clear as the fragments at their feet.

On another occasion, Jeremiah entered the city with a heavy wooden yoke strapped across his shoulders (Jeremiah 27:2). Bent under its weight, he stood before kings and priests, declaring that the nations would bear the yoke of Babylon's rule. The crowd murmured, some shaking their heads in disbelief. Yet the image burned in their memory long after the prophet walked away.

God designed Jeremiah with a purpose already in mind. His role was not an accident or a fallback taken because no one else would do it; it was a calling that aligned with the way God had shaped him.

Confirmation of the call

Most Sunday school teachers will not be called to public acts as dramatic as Jeremiah's, yet the pattern remains. What God is forming often begins quietly, beneath the surface, long before it is recognized or understood. When that formation begins to surface, it does not always arrive with clarity or confidence. More often, it comes with questions, hesitation, and even resistance. Jeremiah reminds us that confirmation does not always bring immediate assurance.

God saw Jeremiah as a chosen prophet before he even entered the world: *"Before I formed you in the womb I knew you; before you were born I sanctified you…"* (Jeremiah 1:5). Yet Jeremiah struggled to see himself that way. He wrestled with feelings of inadequacy, insisting he was too young and too unskilled in speech for the assignment: *"Ah, Lord God! Behold, I cannot speak, for I am a youth"* (Jeremiah 1:6).

According to scholars, Jeremiah spoke this way because he was comparing himself to others. He came from a priestly family and may have felt he did not measure up to those around him. What God saw as preparation, Jeremiah at first saw as disqualification. Yet notice God's response. He did not allow Jeremiah's insecurity to excuse him from the call: *"Do not say, 'I am a youth,' for you shall go to all to whom I send you, and whatever I command you, you shall speak. Do not be afraid of their faces, for I am with you to deliver you, says the Lord*" (Jeremiah 1:7-8). God touched Jeremiah's mouth and said, "*...Behold, I have put My words in your mouth*" (v. 9).

Even with divine confirmation, Jeremiah struggled to see himself as capable of what God had called him to do. His story reminds us that reluctance does not negate calling; often, it accompanies it.

Formation alone, however, is not enough. At some point, the gift of teaching must be acknowledged. As Parker Palmer wisely observed, "The call to teach does not come from encounters alone; no outward teacher or teaching will have much effect until my soul assents." In other words, no matter what others see in us, the calling to teach takes root only when we accept it inwardly.

Similarly, Dr Myles Munroe once said, "Your destiny is decided by God, but the fulfillment is up to you." What others have recognized in us begins to resonate within our own hearts. As we look back over our lives, patterns emerge, moments, experiences, and opportunities that reveal how God has been forming the teacher within. What once felt like a simple talent or natural ability begins to carry greater weight and responsibility. In that moment, we move from unawareness to acknowledgment: *"Yes, teaching is the gift God has placed within me."* It is no longer just what I do; it is who God has called me to be. Jesus Himself set the example. He told His disciples, *"You call me Teacher and Lord, and you say well, for so I am"* (John 13:13).

The uniqueness of the teaching gift

Once the call to teach is recognized and accepted, one of the great joys that follows is discovering that the gift is expressed uniquely in each person. No two teachers carry this calling in the same way, because God shapes both the gift and the Sunday school teacher with intentional care.

That shaping is deeply personal, formed through each individual's identity, culture, upbringing, life experiences, and even challenges. A teacher who grew up in the rural South may use images of farming or family traditions to bring lessons to life. At the same time, someone raised in the city may draw on stories of neighborhoods, schools, or community struggles. A teacher who has walked through illness, grief, or financial hardship may teach with a depth of compassion that others, whose experiences differ, may not carry in the same way. Even mistakes and failures become part of how we teach, providing empathy and patience for those who struggle. In this way, every teacher reflects the handiwork of God through the lens of their own story.

We see this clearly in Scripture. Paul's teaching was shaped by his background as a Pharisee, trained under Gamaliel (Acts 22:3). His letters are filled with careful arguments, references to the Hebrew Scriptures, and structured reasoning that reflect his scholarly upbringing. In contrast, Peter's teaching carried the boldness and simplicity of a fisherman (Acts 4:13). He spoke with a directness that people of his time could understand, often drawing from his personal encounters with Jesus. Both men taught profound lessons, yet their teaching carried different tones and emphases because God had uniquely formed each of them. God uses personality, life history, and experience to give each teaching voice its own expression.

The same diversity of teaching voices is evident not only in individual teachers like Peter and Paul, but also within the Scriptures themselves. The Gospels of Matthew, Mark, and John all tell the story of Jesus. All three walked with Him, witnessed His miracles, and heard His teaching. And yet, each writes differently. This is not a flaw in Scripture; it is the uniqueness of their gift. If we could see them teach what they wrote, the uniqueness would be even clearer.

Matthew writes with a deep awareness of Jewish tradition, frequently connecting Jesus to Old Testament prophecy. His experience as a Jewish believer shapes the way he addresses his audience, presenting Jesus as the promised Messiah. Mark writes with urgency and action, often moving swiftly from one event to the next. John, writing later, reflects on the meaning of Jesus' words and identity, emphasizing relationship, belief, and abiding in Christ.

All three are telling the same story. All three are faithful witnesses. Yet their experiences with Jesus shape what they emphasize, how they frame events, and the language they use. This diversity within unity reminds us that God does not waste life experiences when He calls people to teach. Instead, He uses it.

Another way God prepares the Sunday School teacher is through the teachers who shaped us along the way. Have you ever considered that God may have ordered your steps so you would sit under a particular teacher, whether one who modeled effective teaching or one who revealed areas where a different approach was needed? Even when we are not yet teaching, God forms our instincts through how we learn, listen, and receive care from others.

I was reminded of this truth during a powerful workshop I recently attended, facilitated by a woman whose heart was profoundly shaped by the Lord and by her experience with fellow veterans. During the session, she invited us into a scenario. She said, "Imagine you are a counselor at a summer camp. You have finally lain down to rest when a youth knocks on your door and says, 'I want to go home.' How would you respond? What would you say?"

The room grew quiet as people reflected. One attendee responded, "I would tell them it will be okay, they are alright." Another said, "I would ask them why they want to go home." Both responses were sincere. Both came from a place of care. Yet they were different.

The facilitator then offered a profound insight: most of us respond the way we would want someone to respond to us. Some people long for reassurance and encouragement: "It's going to be okay." Others long to be heard and understood: "Tell me why." Our responses are shaped by our own needs, histories, and the ways we have learned to engage, guide, and support others.

This insight translates directly into teaching. Teachers often teach the way they themselves were taught, the way they learn best, or the way they wish someone had taught them. Some teachers emphasize encouragement and affirmation, while others focus on dialogue and exploration. Some lean toward structure, while others gravitate toward storytelling. None of these approaches is inherently wrong. The danger lies not in the differences, but in assuming that one approach fits everyone.

This same principle applies to Sunday school teachers. No two teachers have walked the same road, encountered God in the same way, or been shaped by the same experiences. Backgrounds, struggles, joys, wounds, callings, and encounters with God all contribute to how we teach. Rather than attempting to imitate another teacher's style or voice, faithful teachers learn to offer God what they uniquely bring to the classroom.

The purpose behind the gift of teaching

The gift of teaching is given not for personal recognition, but for service to the body of Christ. Its purpose is to help Christians grow in understanding, maturity, and faith. Ephesians 4:12 (KJV) tells us clearly, *"for the perfecting of the saints, for the work of the ministry, for the edifying of the body of Christ."* This verse reveals the purpose behind the gift of teaching. The phrase "for the perfecting of the saints" refers to the equipping and maturing of believers. A Sunday school teacher is like a coach in the classroom, equipping students with the tools, knowledge, and confidence to live out their faith. When you teach, you place resources into the hands of God's people that they carry with them long after the lesson ends.

"For the work of the ministry" reminds us that equipping is not merely head knowledge, but action. Ministry is not limited to the classroom; it happens in homes, workplaces, schools, and communities. Your teaching prepares students to minister wherever God has placed them, sharing the gospel, showing compassion, and bearing witness in their everyday lives. Teaching becomes a launching pad that propels others into their callings.

"For the edifying of the body of Christ" refers to the building up of the church, both spiritually and numerically. The word "edifying" means to strengthen, encourage, and construct, promoting growth in Christian wisdom. Sunday school teachers contribute to the church's growth by instilling sound doctrine, deepening understanding of Scripture, and nurturing spiritual maturity. A church without a strong teaching ministry is like a building without a foundation: weak and unstable. Teaching strengthens the body of Christ, ensuring that believers are prepared to stand firm in their faith.

The purpose of the gift of teaching is threefold: to equip the saints, to send them into ministry, and to build up the church. Central to this calling is helping others understand the Word of God.

I recall attending a Vacation Bible School where a man stood and said, "I don't read my Bible because I don't understand the 'thou' and the 'thee.' While some might have dismissed his comment, we were grateful that he had come. His honesty opened the door for conversation, questions, and the beginning of a journey toward understanding.

Teachers may be surprised to discover that many people come to Sunday school not because they lack interest, but because they lack understanding. This was also true in the ministry of Jesus. In Matthew chapter 13, after

Jesus taught the crowds using parables, the disciples approached Him privately and asked for an explanation: "*And the disciples came, and said unto him, Why do You speak to them in parables?*" (v. 10). Their question reveals an essential truth about teaching. Teaching must include understanding. Jesus does not simply repeat the parable. He explains it. He moves from story to meaning, from imagery to insight:

> *"Therefore hear the parable of the sower. When anyone hears the word of the kingdom, and does not understand it, then the wicked one comes and snatches away what was sown in his heart. This is he who received seed by the wayside. But he who received the seed on stony places, this is he who hears the word and immediately receives it; yet he has no root in himself but endures only for a while. For when tribulation or persecution arises because of the word, immediately he stumbles. Now he who received seed among the thorns is he who hears the word, and the cares of this world, and the deceitfulness of riches choke the word, and he becomes unfruitful. But he who received seed on the good ground is he who hears the word and understands it, who indeed bears fruit and produces: some a hundredfold, some sixty, some thirty."* (Matthew 13:18-23).

By explaining the parable to His disciples, Jesus demonstrated that teaching is not complete when words are spoken; it is complete when understanding is formed. His willingness to pause, clarify, and interpret reveals the heart of the teaching gift, guiding others toward comprehension, growth, and faithful response.

The purpose of teaching, then, is not to impress or perform, but to serve, to equip Christians with understanding, to prepare them for ministry, and to strengthen the body of Christ. Teaching moves God's people from confusion to clarity, from curiosity to conviction, and from hearing to living out the Word. When teachers follow the example of Jesus, they recognize that explanation is an act of care, patience, and love. It is through this steady, faithful work that the church is built up and Christians are nurtured toward growth. Yet while the purpose of teaching is outwardly focused on the growth of others, the journey of teaching is also inward, shaping the teacher's own heart, attentiveness, and dependence on God.

The weight and responsibility of the calling to teach

Teaching is not only a gift; it is a responsibility that carries weight. Those who are called to teach Sunday school are entrusted with shaping understanding, guiding faith, and handling the Word of God with care. Scripture reminds us that teaching is never casual or lighthearted, because what is taught has the power to form lives. As we examine the call to teach more closely, we are reminded that this calling involves both joy and weight, obedience and humility, and a deep awareness of the responsibility placed upon those who speak and teach the Word.

Scripture speaks plainly about the seriousness of teaching. James cautions Christians: *"My brethren, let not many of you become teachers, knowing that we shall receive a stricter judgment"* (James 3:1). Teaching places one in a position of influence and accountability, requiring humility, careful discernment, and dependence on God. This warning does not mean teaching is reserved only for the ordained, credentialed, or professionally trained, nor was it intended to discourage teachers. Rather, it reminds them that their words matter and that their influence carries a lasting impact. When this weight is fully realized, it can shape how teachers see themselves and how they place expectations upon themselves.

For some Sunday school teachers, this awareness of responsibility can quietly give rise to a desire for perfection. I recall a season in my own journey when I discovered that I also had the gift of administration. I remember attending a Sunday school teachers' meeting and finding myself more focused on the agenda than on the facilitator. My mind drifted to details that should be centered on the page, to sentences missing a period, to thoughts like how this would stand out more if it were bold.

What began as a growing awareness of responsibility slowly became a pattern in my life. I felt pressure to say everything correctly, to teach flawlessly, and to meet every expectation. I spent countless hours trying to perfect a speech, a lesson, or a presentation, convinced that excellence meant flawlessness. Eventually, worn down by my own self-criticism, I was reminded of the words spoken to the apostle Paul: *And he said unto me, "My grace is sufficient for you, for my strength is made perfect in weakness"* (2 Corinthians 12:9). In that moment, I realized that God had never asked me to be perfect. Teaching does not grow through perfection, but through faithfulness. God does not call Sunday school teachers to be flawless. He calls them to be available, teachable, and willing to grow. It is grace that provides the space in which our gifts are meant to operate.

This tension between weakness and calling, between grace and responsibility, is not unique; it appears throughout Scripture. Jeremiah's story offers a powerful example of a prophet who was called by God yet deeply aware of his own limitations. Even after acknowledging that he was chosen by God, Jeremiah discovered that carrying the message of the Lord was not easy. The calling demanded time, endurance, and a willingness to pour himself out for others. At times, the weight of speaking God's word pressed heavily upon him.

Teaching is sometimes experienced in this way. It requires study, preparation, and persistence, much of which remains unseen. The work can feel heavy, not because the call is unclear, but because the responsibility is real. Yet when the gift has been placed within a person, nothing else truly satisfies until that calling is being lived out. I believe the best feeling in the world is operating in one's calling.

Jeremiah reached a moment when the burden felt overwhelming. He resolved that he would no longer speak for God. Yet even then, the call could not be contained.

> *"Then I said, 'I will not make mention of Him, nor speak anymore in His name.' But His word was in my heart like a burning fire shut up in my bones; I am weary of holding it back, and I could not"*
> (Jeremiah 20:9)

Jeremiah's experience reveals the nature of a God-given teaching call. It is not merely a task one takes on, but a responsibility that presses from within. For those called to teach, the message does not fade simply because the work becomes difficult. It surfaces in conversations, convictions, and the persistent urging of the Spirit to speak the Word of God when silence would be easier. Like a fire shut up in the bones, the call compels the Sunday school teacher to impart what has been entrusted to them.

This inner compulsion to teach ultimately points beyond the individual to a larger purpose.

Jesus made this clear in His final words to His disciples. Before ascending to heaven, He closes His instructions with both a command and a promise. After commissioning them to teach: *"Go therefore, and make disciples of all nations…..teaching them to observe all things that I have commanded you.."* (Matthew 28:19-20) Jesus assures them of His abiding presence: *"and lo, I am with you always, even to the end of the age"* (Matthew 28:19-20). Teaching is not an optional add-on to discipleship; it is a core expression of it.

The beauty of the gift of teaching lies in His promise. Teaching is sustained not by human strength, preparation, or confidence alone, but by the presence of Christ Himself. Those called to teach do not bear the responsibility in isolation; they teach with the assurance that Christ accompanies them, guides them, and remains present in their work. His presence provides endurance when strength wanes and clarity when words fail.

So, who teaches the Sunday school teacher? The gift within. The greatest teacher training program is already underway, shaped and sustained by God's hand. He has entrusted us with a gift that cannot be ignored, silenced, or set aside because it is formed by His hand and confirmed by His call.

Thank you, Sam H. Hairston, dad, for embodying great dedication as my first student.

CHAPTER FOUR:
Formed By The Discipline Of Studying God's Word

Sister Smith's words echoed through the small, sunlit classroom each week, a mantra that lingered in the air alongside the dust motes drifting through the afternoon light. The "us" she spoke of was the teachers of her kindergarten class, a motley crew of enthusiastic volunteers, including myself.

While I could not speak for my fellow teachers, her directive struck a chord deep within me. It became a personal challenge, a promise I made to myself that I would take her words literally. Each evening, as the sun dipped below the horizon and the world quieted, I transformed my humble dining room into a miniature study hall. Commentaries sprawled across the table like open books of wisdom, Bible dictionaries lined up like soldiers ready for battle, and my notepad brimmed with diligent notes. I examined every verse with the precision of a surgeon. I explored the history of the texts, traced the authors' footsteps, and investigated the meanings of words in Greek and Hebrew as if they held the keys to a hidden treasure. I was consumed, poring over Scripture with an insatiable hunger, as though my very soul depended on it.

But every Sunday, as I stood before a classroom of bright-eyed six-year-olds, the reality of my task struck me. I had to distill all that knowledge, all that effort, into something they could grasp. "God, help me to take what I have learned and break it down so a six-year-old can understand," I would whisper under my breath. Somehow, through the Holy Spirit and sheer determination, it happened. I managed to weave intricate theological concepts into relatable stories, engaging games, and vivid illustrations that captured their imaginations.

Yet in those three years, despite my fervent preparation, I never had the opportunity to teach adults. Reflecting on that time, I realized the journey of study was invaluable. I was not merely preparing for a classroom but equipping myself for a lifetime of learning. Sister Smith's words were not just a directive; they were a divine whisper, planting a seed that would grow into a deep hunger for the Word of God. Her challenge was not only about teaching but about transformation. It was about being drawn into the depths of God's Word, not to recite knowledge, but to be changed by it.

The charge to study

When I reflect on my diligence in preparing to teach, I hear Paul's voice echoing from a prison cell, urging his young protégé Timothy: *"Study to shew thyself approved unto God, a workman that needeth not to be ashamed, rightly dividing the word of truth"* (2 Timothy 2:15, KJV)

This single verse is not merely a gentle reminder; it is a charge, a command, a lifeline for those entrusted with God's Word. Paul's words are charged with urgency, shaped by the gravity of his circumstances. The gospel had to be carried forward, and Timothy, his spiritual son, was the one entrusted with the torch. Every word Paul wrote bore the weight of legacy, urgency, and expectation.

Paul begins with "study." The word itself evokes images of sweat on the brow, pages worn thin, and late nights spent in pursuit of truth. Timothy was not instructed to study for personal enrichment. He was pastoring the church at Ephesus, leading a congregation surrounded by competing voices, false teachers, and cultural pressures. Timothy could not lead on talent alone; his youth left him vulnerable to criticism, and his inexperience left him exposed. But Paul reminded him, *"Let no one despise your youth; but be an example of the believers, in word, in conduct, in love, in spirit, in faith, in purity…."* (1 Timothy 4:12). Paul's words remind us that spiritual maturity is not measured by age, but by the depth of God's Word in our lives. Timothy's strength as a young leader was not found in titles or years of experience, but in the Word that had taken root in him through study and devotion. Studying the Word of God plants it in your heart so it is ready to flow out when you speak and teach. When the Word is alive in us, it does not remain on the page; it shows up in our words, our actions, and the way we live.

Then comes the phrase, *"to shew thyself approved by God."* This was not about impressing the elders at Ephesus or silencing critics with clever words. Timothy's preparation was an offering to God Himself. Sunday school teachers today must remember the same: our approval is not measured by human applause but by the grace of the One who sees in secret. When we have labored faithfully in His Word, we can enter the classroom with the quiet confidence that God has already said, "Well done."

Paul then adds, *"a workman that needeth not to be ashamed, rightly dividing the word of truth."* Paul knew what it meant to mishandle the Word of God. He had once been a Pharisee, zealous for the law, confident in his own knowledge, and yet blind to the truth of Christ. His encounter with Jesus on the Damascus Road forever transformed his perspective. From that moment on, Paul understood that knowing the Scriptures was not enough; one had to interpret and apply them rightly. His personal history shaped his charge to Timothy. He was not merely saying, "read the Bible." He was saying, study it with precision, handle it carefully, like an artisan at his bench, measuring twice, cutting once, producing work that can withstand inspection.

The stakes were high for Timothy, and they remain high for us. A false teacher could mislead the congregation. A shallow teacher can weaken the faith of believers. A careless teacher can distort the gospel. But a faithful Sunday school teacher, grounded in Scripture, can strengthen the body of Christ for generations to come.

This call to study echoes into our lives as Sunday school teachers today. Like Timothy, we are entrusted with people who depend on us: children with curious minds, youth wrestling with identity and faith, and adults searching for guidance and wisdom. They are surrounded by the competing voices of culture, media, and peers. If we are not diligent in our study, we risk feeding them our own ideas rather than God's Word. But when we devote ourselves to the Word, when we wrestle with its meaning, and when we seek the guidance of the Holy Spirit in our preparation, we become *"workmen approved by God."* Our approval is not measured by class size, applause, or compliments after the lesson; it is measured by our faithfulness to the text and to the God who gave it.

Remember, studying is not busy work; it is sacred work. It is the process by which God first shapes us so that we can, in turn, shape others. Paul's words to Timothy remind us that teaching is more than an activity; it is a divine trust. To stand before a class with an open Bible is to step into the same line of responsibility Paul entrusted to Timothy. The Sunday school teacher today, like Timothy then, is called to prepare diligently, to divide the Word rightly, and to serve as a faithful steward of God's Word. In doing so, we reflect the heart of Paul's charge, ensuring that our teaching strengthens, equips, and builds up the body of Christ.

While teachers are called to prepare, study, and steward God's Word faithfully, the heart of Christian teaching rests on a profound assurance: God supplies what we cannot produce on our own. Jesus promised His followers, *"But the Helper, the Holy Spirit, whom the Father will send in my name, He will teach you all things and bring to your remembrance all things that I said to you"* (John 14:26). For those called to teach, that promise continues to breathe life into our classrooms today. The Holy Spirit not only enlightens our understanding as we study but also recalls the Word when we need it most, whether we stand before curious minds, respond to difficult questions, or guide learners through moments of doubt. When opinions rise, and uncertainty lingers, the Spirit whispers reminders of what God has already said. That is why our preparation matters. The Spirit draws from what has already been planted in us; He can bring to remembrance only what we have taken the time to study.

Paul – Studying Scripture in light of Christ

Let us look more closely at the Apostle Paul. Before Paul ever planted churches, mentored leaders, or wrote letters, he was first a student of Scripture. Trained in the Hebrew Scriptures and deeply immersed in Israel's story, Paul did not abandon rigorous study when he encountered Christ on the road to Damascus; he reoriented it. His conversion did not negate his learning; it transformed the lens through which he read. Paul's careful, disciplined engagement with Scripture became the foundation for everything he later wrote and taught. His letters reveal a mind shaped by sustained study, one that reads attentively, remembers deeply, and interprets Scripture through the light of Christ.

Paul's study of Scripture is evident not only in what he teaches, but in how he teaches. He does not offer disconnected ideas or isolated proof texts; instead, he traces themes, connects narratives, and rereads Israel's Scriptures through Christ. Through careful reading and theological reflection, Paul shows how the promises, failures, and hopes of the Hebrew Scriptures find their fulfillment in Jesus Christ. His writings invite believers to see themselves within God's redemptive story, not by abandoning Scripture, but by engaging it more deeply through the revelation of Christ.

One of Paul's clearest examples of Scripture-shaped teaching is his presentation of Christ as the second Adam. Drawing from the creation and fall narratives in Genesis 2:15, "*Then the Lord God took the man, and put him in the garden of Eden to tend and keep it*," and 3:24, "*So he drove out the man; and He placed cherubim at the east of the garden of Eden, and a flaming sword which turned every way, to guard the way to the tree of life.*" Paul demonstrates a careful reading of the text and its theological implications. Adam, placed within a good and ordered creation, failed to live in faithful obedience to God, introducing sin and death into the human story. Paul does not merely retell this account; he studies it, reflects on it, and then rereads it through Christ. In Romans 5:12-21, Paul carefully contrasts that through Adam came sin and death, but through Christ came righteousness and life:

> *Therefore, just as through one man sin entered the world, and death through sin, and thus death spread to all men, because all sinned……. For the judgment which came from one offense resulted in condemnation, but the free gift which came from many offenses resulted in justification. For if by the one man's offense death reigned through the one, much more those who receive abundance of grace and of the gift of righteousness will reign in life through the One, Jesus Christ. Therefore, as*

through one man's offense judgment came to all men, resulting in condemnation, even so through one Man's righteous act the free gift came to all men, resulting in justification of life. For as by one man's disobedience many were made sinners, so also by one Man's obedience many will be made righteous. Moreover the law entered that the offense might abound. But where sin abounded, grace abounded much more, so that as sin reigned in death, even so grace might reign through righteousness to eternal life through Jesus Christ our Lord.

This is not a casual interpretation; it is the work of a trained mind steeped in Scripture. Paul extends this study further in 1 Corinthians 15:20-23:

"But now is Christ is risen from the dead, and has become the firstfruits of those who have fallen asleep. For since by man came death, by Man also came the resurrection of the dead. For as in Adam all die, even so in Christ all shall be made alive. But each one in his own order: Christ the firstfruits, afterward those who are Christ's at his coming."

He presents Christ as the "first fruits" of the resurrection, reversing the curse of death introduced through Adam. His teaching flows directly from sustained engagement with the Hebrew Scriptures, demonstrating how faithful study equips the teacher to write clearly, teach wisely, and guide others into deeper understanding.

Stephen – A student of the Word

Paul's example reminds us that faithful teaching begins with disciplined study; Stephen shows us what that study looks like when Scripture lives not only on scrolls, but in the heart and on the tongue.

Stephen appears in the early church as one of the first deacons, chosen to serve because he was *"full of faith and the Holy Spirit"* (Acts 6:5). Though appointed for service, Stephen quickly became known for his powerful proclamation of God's Word. He boldly engaged in theological debate, interpreting Israel's history through the revelation of Jesus Christ. Imagine him standing before the Sanhedrin, surrounded by angry faces, listening to false accusations, the air thick with tension. Though the room was filled with hostility, Stephen stood calm and unafraid. The Word of God was alive within him, burning brighter than the fury around him. When he opened his mouth, the Scriptures poured out like a river as he recounted the story of Abraham, Moses, Joseph, David, and the prophets. Scripture testifies, *"And they were not able to resist the wisdom and the spirit by which he spake"* (Acts 6:10).

Stephen did not reach for scrolls or notes, and his words were not a memorized speech. The Word had become part of him long before that moment, living within him through years of listening, learning, and devotion. In that final hour, the Spirit drew from what was already planted inside him, bringing the Scriptures to his remembrance and granting him the boldness to speak about Jesus, even in the face of death.

Ezra – A studied Teacher

Stephen demonstrates the power of an internalized Word, while Ezra embodies the disciplined study required to teach and reform God's people faithfully. Ezra emerges in Scripture as a priest, scribe, and reformer during the postexilic period of Israel's history. Living after the Babylonian exile, Ezra belonged to the generation tasked with restoring not only the physical structures of Jerusalem, but also the spiritual identity of God's people. Scripture gives us a portrait of this devoted teacher: *"For Ezra had prepared his heart to seek the Law of the Lord, and to do it, and to teach His statutes and ordinances in Israel"* (Ezra 7:10).

Before he ever stood behind a scroll to read it, he stood before God. His study was not casual or merely academic; it was an act of worship. Ezra had set his heart first to understand the words on the scroll, then to live them, and only then to teach them. In the book of Ezra, we see that true teaching flows from a life already shaped by God's Word.

When the people later gathered at the Water Gate (Nehemiah 8:1–9), it was Ezra who read aloud from the

Book of the Law, from dawn until noon. Imagine the scene: the crowd standing, hands lifted, tears streaming, as the Scriptures pierced their hearts. What began in one man's private study ignited public renewal. The same Scriptures that had shaped Ezra's life now shaped a nation. As Ezra read and explained the Scriptures, the people understood, repented, and turned their hearts back to God. His disciplined study transformed information into formation, preparing him to lead others with clarity and conviction.

Yet Scripture also shows that God's work of forming teachers does not end with study alone. It continues through lived experience, failure, restoration, and the empowering work of the Spirit.

Peter – When study meets the Spirit

Peter, originally a fisherman from Galilee, stands as a powerful example of how God forms teachers through lived experience. Unlike Ezra's scholarly background or Stephen's eloquent speech, Peter's early life was marked by impulsiveness, bold declarations, and notable failures, including his denial of Jesus. Yet it was precisely through these experiences that Peter was shaped into a faithful teacher of the early church. That formation comes into full view on the day of Pentecost.

He now stood before a crowd in Jerusalem (Acts 2). The wind of Pentecost had barely settled when thousands rushed in to see and hear what was happening. The atmosphere was thick with questions, wonder, and disbelief: *"So they were all amazed, and perplexed, saying to one another, Whatever could this mean? Other mocking said, they are full of new wine."* (Acts 2:12-13)

Yet Peter, no longer the man who once stumbled for words, stood up filled with the Spirit and spoke with confidence. Without hesitation, he reached for the Scriptures, his voice carrying above the noise:

> *"But this is what was spoken by the prophet Joel: 'And it shall come to pass in the last days, says God, That I will pour out of My Spirit on all flesh; Your sons and your daughters shall prophesy, Your young men shall see visions, Your old men shall dream dreams"* (Acts 2:16-17).

In an instant, years of walking with Jesus, of listening, questioning, and learning, rose to the surface. The Holy Spirit did not give Peter new words to speak; He illuminated the Scriptures already within him. What had once been preparation now became proclamation.

From Paul's charge to Timothy to "study to show yourself approved," Scripture consistently affirms that faithful teaching flows from deliberate preparation. Paul himself modeled this diligence, drawing from the Hebrew Scriptures as he wrote, taught, and proclaimed the gospel.

Stephen stands as a witness to a Word so fully internalized that it required no notes, only obedience and courage. Ezra demonstrates the sacred work of a teacher whose disciplined study led not merely to knowledge, but to repentance and renewal among God's people. Finally, Peter reveals the culmination of this journey: what had been formed through learning, failure, restoration, and Spirit-led shaping now burst forth in bold proclamation. Together, these witnesses remind us that teaching in Sunday school is neither accidental nor merely intellectual. It is a holy calling shaped by study, sustained by the Holy Spirit, and ultimately expressed through faithful proclamation for the building up of the body of Christ.

Perhaps the Sunday school teacher training program is not found in a classroom or written in a manual but formed each time we open the Scriptures. When we study the Word, the Holy Spirit trains us from within, ready to bring the Scriptures forth at the right time. The greatest teacher training may already be taking place within us, as we study scriptures, quietly facilitated by God Himself.

 Thank you, Sis. Smith, for inspiring me to study, laying the foundation that has shaped my walk with God, and my call to teach.

CHAPTER FIVE:

Formed In Relationship: Learning From Those We Teach

"A man's gift maketh room for him, and bringeth him before great men" (Proverbs 18:16)

It was a Sunday morning when I first walked into Second Baptist Church. The moment I stepped into the education wing, I sensed the movement of the Holy Spirit. The open doors of the Sunday school classrooms revealed a world of variety and possibility. Each room seemed to tell its own story, speaking silently before a single word was taught.

There were five adult classrooms, and students had the freedom to choose which one they would attend. Their choice often came down to where they felt most at ease, which room fit their comfort, their rhythm, even their way of connecting. One classroom featured a large round table where students sat face to face, creating an intimate circle that invited open conversation. Down the hall, another was arranged in neat rows, giving a sense of order and formality. A third classroom had tables arranged in a square, a balancing structure with connection, where students could look across at one another as they shared their stories.

The differences did not stop with the furniture. Some teachers stood confidently at the front, filling the room with their energy, while others chose to sit among their students, creating a conversational feel. In one room, a teacher used PowerPoint slides to emphasize the lesson, while in another, the discussion flowed straight from open Bibles and thoughtful questions. Neither method was better than the other; they reflected the teacher's style and allowed students to choose what resonated with them.

Even the atmosphere varied. One classroom had Scriptures pinned to the walls, serving as constant reminders of God's Word. Another displayed colorful banners and artwork, making the room warm and inviting. In a few rooms, teachers had coffee brewing in the corner, filling the space with the aroma of hospitality. The size of the rooms communicated something different as well. One felt cozy and intimate, while another was large and airy, offering a sense of freedom and openness. Each space, whether intentionally or not, was already teaching before any lesson began.

The environment we create matters because it becomes the setting in which God places those entrusted to our care. Proverbs 18:16 reminds us that *"A man's gift makes room for him, and brings him before great men,"* suggesting that God opens doors for those He has gifted and positions them before greatness. For the Sunday school teacher, that greatness is often found in the very people who enter the classroom. More often than not, learners arrive not only to receive instructions, but to participate in God's ongoing work of formation, shaping the teacher even as they are being taught. The classroom becomes one of the primary spaces in which God continues forming the teacher. From the moment students enter, teachers are shaped by what they see in the faces before them, by what they feel as they encounter the emotions others carry, and by how carefully they listen to voices entrusted to their care.

Formed by what we see

Walking through those classrooms at Second Baptist reminded me that space speaks. What learners see silently communicates whether they belong, whether this will be a place of connection or distance, and whether learning will feel rigid or alive. Scripture reminds us that seeing can do even more; it can interrupt the ordinary and reshape how a person understands themselves and their calling. Moses experienced such a moment on what began as an ordinary day, tending his flock on the far side of the wilderness. Then, out of the corner of his eye, he noticed something unusual: a bush engulfed in fire that refused to be consumed. Curiosity pulled him closer, unaware that this visual interruption would forever change how he understood who he was and what God was calling him to do:

> *"Now Moses was tending the flock of Jethro his father-in-law, the priest of Midian. And he led the flock to the back of the desert, and came to Horeb, the mountain of God. And the Angel of the Lord appeared to him in a flame of fire from the midst of a bush. So he looked, and behold, the bush was burning with fire, but the bush was not consumed. Then Moses said, "I will now turn aside and see this great sight, why the bush does not burn."*
> (Exodus 3:1-3)

The dust clung to his feet as he stepped nearer, and in that moment, the desert became a sanctuary. What he saw changed the posture of his heart, preparing him to hear the voice of God:

> *"So when the Lord saw that he turned aside to look, God called to him from the midst of the bush and said, "Moses, Moses!" And he said, "Here I am." Then He said, "Do not draw near this place. Take your sandals off your feet, for the place where you stand is holy ground "*(Exodus 3:4-5)

Isaiah's encounter echoes the same interruption, but with even greater intensity. In the year that King Uzziah died, Isaiah entered the temple carrying the weight of national uncertainty and personal grief. What he saw there shattered every ordinary frame of reference:

> *"In the year that King Uzziah died, I saw the Lord sitting on a throne, high and lifted up, and the train of His robe filled the temple. Above it stood seraphim; each one had six wings: with two he covered his face, with two he covered his feet, and with two he flew. And one cried to another and said: "Holy, holy, holy is the Lord of hosts; The whole earth is full of His glory!" And the posts of the door were shaken by the voice of him who cried out, and the house was filled with smoke"* (Isaiah 6:1-4)

This sight redefined Isaiah's understanding of himself. Confronted by God's holiness, he saw his own unworthiness with painful clarity and cried out, *"So said I, Woe is me, for I am undone! Because I am a man of unclean lips, And I dwell in the midst of a people of unclean lips; For my eyes have seen the King, The Lord of hosts"* (Isaiah 6:5). Through cleansing and divine initiative, his vision moved from confession to calling: *"Also I heard the voice of the Lord saying: "Whom shall I send, and who will go for Us? Then said I, Here am I! Send me"* (Isaiah 6:8). The moment he saw God in His holiness, Isaiah began to understand himself differently, not merely as an observer of God, but as one invited into God's redemptive work.

Moses and Isaiah together remind teachers that seeing is never neutral. What we see has the power to interrupt routine, reshape identity, and awaken calling. In the Sunday school classroom, teachers are continually being shaped by what they see, not only the physical environment but also the people God places before them. Teachers learn to see curiosity awaken in the hesitant question, resilience emerge from a painful story, and faith take root in small, ordinary moments. They also learn to see what is easily overlooked: silent struggle, guarded hope or the quiet readiness of a learner who has not yet spoken. Over time, God trains the teacher's eyes to notice growth before it is fully visible and calling before it is clearly named.

Seeing also shapes teachers inwardly. As teachers witness both limitations and possibilities in those they teach, they often confront their own assumptions, expectations, and dependence on God. Like Moses turning aside to look more closely, teachers are invited to pause, attend, and recognize holy ground in places that once felt ordinary. The classroom becomes a site of revelation, not because teachers manufacture sacred moments, but because God reveals Himself through what is seen when teachers are willing to look attentively. In this way, what teachers see not only informs how they teach; it continues to form who they are becoming as servants called to God's work.

Formed by what we feel

God forms teachers, in part, through the capacity to feel with those entrusted to their care. Scripture affirms this shared emotional life when it calls believers to *"rejoice with those that who rejoice, and weep with those who weep"* (Romans 12:15). Such language assumes that God has created us with the ability to enter into the joys and sorrows of others, not as detached observers, but as companions along the journey of life. In the classroom, teachers often sense celebration in a learner's breakthrough, heaviness in an unspoken struggle, and discouragement beneath a hesitant question.

Neuroscience offers language that helps describe this human capacity, pointing to what are often called *mirror neurons* – a system in the brain that allows individuals to internally reflect the emotions and experiences they observe in others. In simple terms, what another person is feeling can, in some measure, be felt within us. If this understanding is correct, it suggests that God has designed us with an embodied ability to come alongside others in their joy, disappointment, fear, and hope. This capacity does not rely on physical touch, but on presence, attentiveness, and relationship. As teachers grow in awareness of what learners carry emotionally, God uses these moments of shared feeling to deepen compassion, sharpen discernment, and continue to form the teacher's heart for the work to which they have been called. Jesus

Himself gives us a vivid example of this, sharing feeling, one that reveals how entering another's sorrow becomes a sacred act of presence rather than a departure from ministry.

The road into Bethany was heavy that day. Grief has a way of slowing footsteps and filling the room with mourning. Word had already spread – Lazarus was dead. Friends and neighbors filled the house, their voices hushed, some weeping openly, others sitting in silence, unsure of what to say. Into this space of sorrow walked Jesus (John 11).

Martha came first, her words a mixture of faith and disappointment: *"Lord if You would have been here, my brother would not have died"* (John 11:21). Jesus listened. He did not rush her grief or correct her theology. He stood with her in the ache of what might have been.

Then Mary came. Unlike her sister, she said nothing more. She fell at His feet, tears spilling onto the dust below, then her body spoke what words could not. The crowd began to weep with her, grief rippling outward like waves. And then something remarkable happened, something expected.

Jesus stopped. He did not lift His hands. He did not speak a command. He did not yet call the dead to rise. Instead, He allowed Himself to feel. John tells us simply, powerfully: *"Jesus wept"* (John 11:35). The Creator of life stood at the edge of death and let tears fall. He felt the sting of loss, the weight of sorrow, and the pain carried by those He loved. Though He knew resurrection was moments away, He did not bypass their grief. He entered it. He allowed their pain to be reflected within Himself.

Those standing nearby noticed. Some whispered. "Behold how he loved him." Others questioned. But what they all witnessed was a Savior who did not remain distant from human suffering. Jesus did not merely observe grief; He shared it. Only after He felt with them did He move toward the miracle.

Formed through hearing

Belonging is not sustained by presence alone; it is deepened through being heard, and teachers are formed in the practice of listening as much as learners are formed in being heard. A classroom may feel warm and welcoming, but when teachers learn to receive voices with care, patience, and intention, belonging is strengthened for everyone present. To hear well is to recognize that thoughts, questions, doubts, and insights carry sacred weight. As teachers listen, they come to understand that voices offered in trust are not interruptions to learning, but invitations into deeper formation. Hearing communicates a powerful message, not only to learners but also to teachers: God is at work here.

In Scripture, listening is often portrayed not simply as a cognitive activity but as a sacred discipline that signals readiness, obedience, and responsibility. This sacred understanding of listening is illustrated in the book of Leviticus. When Moses consecrated Aaron and his sons as priests, the ceremony included a striking and unusual act:

> *"And he brought the second ram, the ram of consecration. Then Aaron and his sons laid their hands on the head of the ram, and Moses killed it. Also he took some of its blood and put it on the tip of Aaron's right ear, on the thumb of his right hand, and on the big toe of his right foot..."*
> (Leviticus 8:22-23).

Pause for a moment and picture the scene. The people of Israel are gathered in silence as Moses carefully anoints the priests. Blood is placed first on the ear, setting it apart for holy service. The ear is consecrated to hear God's Word. Then Moses places the blood on the right hand, setting it apart to do God's work, and finally on the right foot, consecrating it to walk in God's ways. Each act reminds us that listening comes first. Before Aaron could speak for God, he had to hear God. Before he could minister to the people, he had to listen to their cries. The ear, therefore, is not merely a physical organ; it symbolizes the sacred responsibility of listening with intention and compassion.

For teachers, this consecration of the ear reminds us that listening is part of our formation before it ever becomes part of our instruction. Teaching requires more than delivering lessons; it calls for cultivating ears that are attentive, patient, and compassionate. Every whispered comment, hesitant question, and even silence carries meaning. When teachers listen well, students begin to feel safe enough to open their hearts, and it is in this sacred exchange that learning becomes transformation.

In my years as a chaplain, I learned that attentive listening often formed me as much as it helped those I served. Many entered conversations seeking answers, yet as they were given space to speak, clarity often emerged, not because I solved the problem, but because they did. Research in counseling and pastoral care affirms what many teachers intuitively observe: speaking aloud in a safe, attentive environment helps individuals organize their thoughts, reflect more deeply, and discover insights for themselves. Listening, then, is not passive; it is an active, formative practice.

We see this sacred discipline modeled most clearly in the way Jesus entered conversations marked by grief, confusion, and unanswered questions. On the road to Emmaus, two discouraged men walked down a dusty path, their shoulders heavy with sorrow. Their hopes had died with the crucifixion, and their words were soaked in confusion and disappointment. Though they did not recognize Him, Jesus came alongside them and asked a simple question: *"What kind of conversation is this that you have with one another as you walk, and are sad?"* (Luke 24:17). The question was gentle, almost casual, yet it opened the door for their pain to step through. The men stopped in their tracks. He listened as they spoke of crushed hopes and unanswered questions, never interrupting, never correcting, simply walking with them. Only after listening did he open the Scriptures to them (Luke 24:25-27).

His listening prepared their hearts to receive His word. More than that, it reveals something essential about formation: before teachers speak the Word of God, they are shaped by the discipline of listening. The most powerful gift a Sunday school teacher can offer is not a quick answer, but a listening ear. Listening builds trust, softens hearts, and opens space for God's Word to take root. When teachers practice this kind of listening, they are not only serving learners; they are being formed themselves, mirroring the attentiveness of a God who bends His ear toward His people and shaping their own hearts for the sacred work to which they have been called.

From the moment students walk through the door, they are shaped by what they see, how they feel, and what they are invited to share. The space matters. Being noticed matters and being heard matters. Yet each of these is more than a teaching practice; they are part of God's way of forming us as Sunday school teachers. He is not merely developing our skills; He is shaping our hearts to reflect His own through what we see in others, what we hear in their voices, and what we feel as we walk alongside them.

When I first arrived at Second Baptist, I remember asking myself, "*What need do I need to fulfill here?*" I believed that if God had sent me, then surely it was because there was a gap I was meant to fill. But when my season there came to an end, I realized something unexpected. The church and its people had been such a blessing to me that I grieved leaving. I still remember driving down the road with tears in my eyes, coming to understand a deeper truth: I was not sent to Second Baptist because they had a need; I was sent because I had a need. God had placed me in that environment to shape me, to heal me, and to teach me. In that season, I learned that sometimes the most important lessons for a teacher are learned not while speaking, but while listening, watching, and experiencing how God works through His people. He is the Master Teacher, faithfully orchestrating not only where we serve, but how we are being formed.

Perhaps the greatest teacher training program is not found in manuals or methods, but in the moments God has designed to mold us. Every classroom we enter, every student we meet, and every season of service becomes part of their divine lesson plan. Through the people we teach and the places we serve, God is teaching us. And when we begin to see our classrooms, and even our seasons of service, as His classroom for us, we discover that the Master Teacher has been preparing us all along, shaping us not only to teach His Word, but also to reflect His heart.

With deepest gratitude, I thank Pastor William Wyne, Corinne Harter, the Sunday school teachers, and my Second Baptist family of Battle Creek, Michigan, for allowing God to use you as a blessing in my life. My season with you reminded me that God's training often comes through the love, faithfulness, and care of His people.

CONCLUSION:
The Teacher is Still Being Taught

If there is one truth that becomes clear through every chapter of this book, it is this: the Sunday school teacher is never finished learning.

Many people step into a classroom believing they are there only to teach others. They prepare lessons, read Scriptures, gather resources, and stand before learners with the desire to share God's Word faithfully. Yet somewhere along the way, something unexpected happens. The teacher begins to realize that God is also teaching them.

The Master Teacher, Jesus Christ, shows us how teaching transforms lives. His words captured attention, stirred hearts, and invited people to think deeply about the kingdom of God. But Jesus did more than deliver information; He formed people. Those who came into His presence were changed by the experience and by the power of His teaching.

The Holy Spirit continues that same work today. The Spirit helps, reminds, reveals, and guides those who teach

God's Word. When teachers feel unsure, overwhelmed, or unprepared, the Holy Spirit quietly works within them, strengthening their confidence and reminding them that they are never alone in their calling.

God also forms teachers through the gift He has placed within them. Many discover their calling long before they know what to call it. They find themselves explaining scripture, answering questions, encouraging others, and helping people understand the Bible. Over time, the church and others affirm what God has already begun to shape.

But the formation of a teacher does not stop there. Teachers are shaped through the discipline of studying God's Word. Scripture becomes both the message we share and the place where God continues to shape our own hearts. The more we study, the more we realize how much there is still to learn.

Finally, teachers are formed through their relationships with the very people they teach. Students are not simple listeners; they are part of the teacher's formation. Their questions, experiences, struggles, and insights become part of the classroom experience. Often, the teacher learns as much from the learners as the learners do from the teacher.

This is one of the profound truths of serving as a Sunday school teacher: while we are equipping others with God's Word, God is still equipping us.

For those who serve in Sunday school classrooms, Bible study groups, youth ministries, and small group settings, remember this: your willingness to teach matters more than your perfection. Many teachers begin their journey with little training, uncertain of their abilities, but confident in one thing: their love for God, His people, and His Word.

God honors that willingness.

If you are teaching today, continue to listen for the voice of the Master Teacher. Continue to rely on the Holy Spirit. Continue to study God's Word faithfully. And continue to learn from those whom God places in your classroom.

Perhaps the greatest teaching-training program is not a program at all, but a divine process initiated and guided by God Himself.

ABOUT THE AUTHOR

Rev. Dr. Benita K. Hairston-Gorham is a seasoned minister, Christian Educator, and servant-leader with more than forty years of experience walking alongside volunteer Sunday school teachers and church educators. She understands the sacred responsibility carried by those who step into the classroom week after week, often with limited training, but with a deep desire to faithfully teach God's Word.

Throughout her ministry, Dr. Hairston-Gorham has served a wide range of roles within the church, including Associate Minister, Sunday school teacher, superintendent, Dean of a Christian Leadership School of the National Baptist Convention, USA, Inc., Certified Instructor of the Sunday School Publishing Board, Vice President of the District Congress of Christian Education, and Director of Christian Education. These experiences have shaped her conviction that teaching in the church is both a calling and a craft-one that deserves preparation, encouragement, and care.

Her ministry is also informed by years of pastoral presence beyond the classroom. As a retired VA Hospital Chaplain and US Air Force Veteran, she has journeyed with individuals and families through moments of grief, uncertainty, and healing, which deeply influence how she approaches teaching with compassion, attentiveness, and respect for every learner.

Grounded in theological education, Dr. Hairston-Gorham holds a Master of Divinity from Shaw University and a Doctor of Ministry from Campbell University. She is currently pursuing a PhD in Education at Regent University, with a focus on Christian education and online learning. She has also taught as a Professor of Religious Studies, offering courses in World Religions, New Testament, and Old Testament Survey.

With years of formal training and lived ministry experience behind her, Dr. Hairston-Gorham has discovered that while many institutions teach skills, God shapes the teacher. This realization gave rise to *Who is Teaching the Teacher.* This book explores the divine process of preparation and invites readers to consider a profound question: Could the greatest teacher-training program already be in motion, facilitated by God Himself?

Above all, Dr. Benita Hairston-Gorham is a grateful servant of God who believes that no teacher stands in the classroom by accident. She remains committed to encouraging, equipping, and affirming those who teach, helping them recognize that their faithfulness to teaching Sunday School is a sacred calling.

Her lifelong guiding motto is "All Things Christian Education," inspired by 2 Timothy 2:15: *Study to show thyself approved unto God, a workman that needeth not to be ashamed, rightly dividing the word of truth."*

To contact Dr. Hairston-Gorham or learn more about her work in Christian education, you may reach her at info@nbchristianed.com or visit the website: www.nbchristianed.com.